THE WORLD OF OCEAN ANIMALS
ORCAS

by Mari Schuh

pogo

Ideas for Parents and Teachers

Pogo Books let children practice reading informational text while introducing them to nonfiction features such as headings, labels, sidebars, maps, and diagrams, as well as a table of contents, glossary, and index.

Carefully leveled text with a strong photo match offers early fluent readers the support they need to succeed.

Before Reading

- "Walk" through the book and point out the various nonfiction features. Ask the student what purpose each feature serves.
- Look at the glossary together. Read and discuss the words.

Read the Book

- Have the child read the book independently.
- Invite him or her to list questions that arise from reading.

After Reading

- Discuss the child's questions. Talk about how he or she might find answers to those questions.
- Prompt the child to think more. Ask: Orcas are a kind of dolphin. What do you know about dolphins?

Pogo Books are published by Jump!
5357 Penn Avenue South
Minneapolis, MN 55419
www.jumplibrary.com

Library of Congress Cataloging-in-Publication Data

Names: Schuh, Mari C., 1975- author.
Title: Orcas / by Mari Schuh.
Description: Minneapolis, MN: Jump!, Inc., [2022]
Series: The world of ocean animals
Includes index. | Audience: Ages 7–10
Identifiers: LCCN 2020056257 (print)
LCCN 2020056258 (ebook)
ISBN 9781636900636 (hardcover)
ISBN 9781636900643 (paperback)
ISBN 9781636900650 (ebook)
Subjects: LCSH: Killer whale–Juvenile literature.
Classification: LCC QL737.C432 S42883 2022 (print)
LCC QL737.C432 (ebook) | DDC 599.53/6–dc23
LC record available at https://lccn.loc.gov/2020056257
LC ebook record available at https://lccn.loc.gov/2020056258

Editor: Jenna Gleisner
Designer: Michelle Sonnek

Photo Credits: slowmotiongli/Shutterstock, cover, 19; SuperStock, 1; Tory Kallman/Shutterstock, 3; Lazareva/iStock, 4, 12; WaterFrame/Alamy, 5; Nature Picture Library/Alamy, 6-7; Niels Vos/Shutterstock, 8-9; Doug Perrine/Alamy, 10-11; Willyam Bradberry/Shutterstock, 13; Grafissimo/iStock, 14-15; Wolfgang Jakel/imageBROKER/SuperStock, 16-17; MarkMalleson/iStock, 18; by wildestanimal/Getty, 20-21; Tatiana Ivkovich/Shutterstock, 23.

Printed in the United States of America at Corporate Graphics in North Mankato, Minnesota.

TABLE OF CONTENTS

CHAPTER 1

BLACK AND WHITE DOLPHINS

A tall, black dorsal fin sticks out of the ocean. It is six feet (1.8 meters) tall! What does it belong to? An orca!

dorsal fin

Orcas are black and white. Their coloring acts as **camouflage**. How? If an animal looks at an orca from above, its black back blends in with the dark water. If it looks at one from below, the orca's white belly blends in with sunlight shining down from above.

Orcas are a kind of dolphin.
They are the biggest kind.
Adult males can weigh up to
9.9 tons (9,000 kilograms)!
Females can be up to 7.5 tons
(6,800 kg).

DID YOU KNOW?

Orcas are not whales. But they are sometimes called killer whales. Why? Orcas kill and eat many types of whales.

Orcas swim in every ocean in the world. They often swim in cold water near the **coast**. They have layers of **blubber** to keep them warm. They also swim in warm, **tropical** waters.

TAKE A LOOK!

Where do orcas live? Take a look!

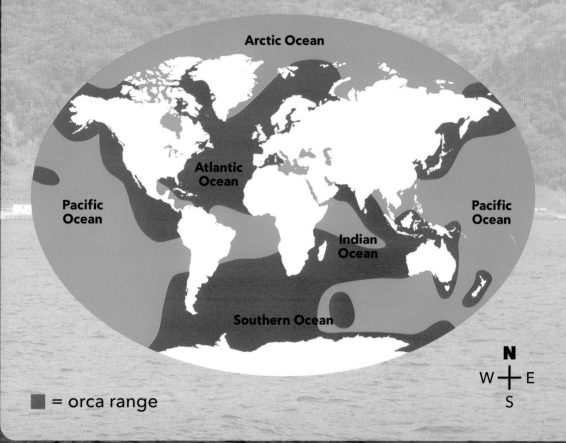

Arctic Ocean

Atlantic
Ocean

Pacific
Ocean

Pacific
Ocean

Indian
Ocean

Southern Ocean

N
W — E
S

■ = orca range

Orcas are fast swimmers! As they swim, they quickly jump out of the water and dive back in. They come up for air and breathe through **blowholes**.

An orca can leap its whole body out of the water. Then it smacks down on the surface. This is called **breaching**. Splash!

breaching

TAKE A LOOK!

Orcas move their flukes up and down to swim. Take a look at an orca's other body parts!

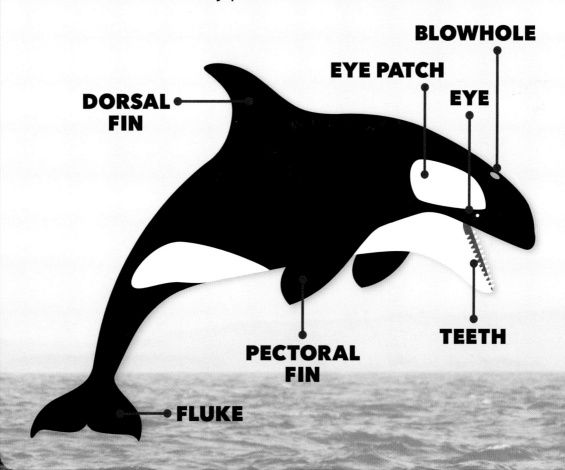

DORSAL FIN

EYE PATCH

BLOWHOLE

EYE

TEETH

PECTORAL FIN

FLUKE

CHAPTER 2
LIFE IN A POD

Orcas live in groups called **pods**. Pods travel and hunt together. They often have fewer than 40 orcas. Older females lead pods.

pod

Pods **migrate** long distances. Some swim to new areas without ice. Others migrate to follow **prey**. Orcas eat fish, seals, penguins, sea lions, and walruses. They also hunt squid, sharks, and whales!

Orcas need about 500 pounds (227 kg) of food a day! They use their sharp teeth to grab and tear prey. They eat some prey in chunks. They swallow others whole!

Orcas are at the top of their **food chain**. No animals hunt orcas. This makes them **apex predators**.

Sometimes, orcas hunt alone. An orca can beach itself to grab a sea lion. Other times, a pod hunts together. They all swim to make big waves. The waves can push a seal off ice and into the water. Mealtime!

CHAPTER 3

ORCA CALVES

Orcas **mate** throughout the year. Like most **mammals**, females give birth to live young. A female gives birth to one **calf** at a time.

calf

Calves are born in the water. They drink their mothers' milk for up to two years. The milk helps them grow blubber.

Mothers take good care of their calves. Other females in the pod help. Calves swim close to their mothers as they grow. They learn how to hunt.

Many young orcas leave their pods to join new pods. Others stay in the same pods their whole lives.

DID YOU KNOW?

Orcas use **echolocation** to help them hunt and travel. They whistle, click, and pop. The sounds travel through the water and hit objects. They bounce back as echoes. The echoes help orcas find food.

ACTIVITIES & TOOLS

CAMOUFLAGE COLORS

An orca's black and white coloring helps it hide in the ocean. Try this activity to see how camouflage works.

What You Need:
- small black objects, such as buttons or beads
- small white objects, such as buttons or beads
- black and white construction paper
- timer or stopwatch
- one friend

❶ Collect small objects that are all black and all white, such as buttons or beads.

❷ Place a black piece of construction paper on a flat surface. Sprinkle the buttons or beads onto the paper.

❸ Set a timer for 10 seconds. Ask your friend to pick out as many black buttons or beads as he or she can.

❹ Your turn! Do the same activity with white paper. How many white buttons can you find in 10 seconds?

GLOSSARY

apex predators: Predators at the top of a food chain that are not hunted by any other animal.

blowholes: Nostrils on the top of whale and dolphin heads that are used for breathing air.

blubber: A thick layer of fat under the skin of some ocean animals.

breaching: Rising and breaking through the surface of the water.

calf: A young orca.

camouflage: A disguise or natural coloring that allows animals to hide by making them look like their surroundings.

coast: The land next to an ocean or sea.

echolocation: The practice of finding objects by using sounds and echoes.

food chain: An ordered arrangement of animals and plants in which each feeds on the one below it in the chain.

mammals: Warm-blooded animals that give birth to live young, which drink milk from their mothers.

mate: To join together to produce young.

migrate: To travel from one place to another place during different times of the year.

pods: Groups of orcas.

prey: Animals that are hunted by other animals for food.

tropical: Of or having to do with the hot, rainy area of the tropics.

INDEX

TO LEARN MORE

Finding more information is as easy as 1, 2, 3.

❶ Go to www.factsurfer.com

❷ Enter "orcas" into the search box.

❸ Choose your book to see a list of websites.

FACT SURFER